You Can Crochet

You Can Crochet

A Comprehensive Guide
Specially Written for the Beginner

Sharon White

Kangaroo Press

Contents

To Peter, Steven and Trevor for their encouragement and total support throughout

Acknowledgement
Photography by Russ Kirkland

© Sharon White 1990

First published in 1990 by Kangaroo Press Pty Ltd
3 Whitehall Road (P.O. Box 75) Kenthurst 2156
Typeset by G.T. Setters Pty Limited
Printed in Singapore by Fong & Sons Printers Pte Ltd

ISBN 0 86417 319 9

Introduction

My book is written for the beginner.

The aim of *You Can Crochet* is to gradually teach you the right way to read a crochet pattern. The patterns in this book are easy to read and simple to understand. I hope my book will give you confidence to eventually read any crochet pattern successfully.

Once you have mastered the first few basic stitches, I know you will enjoy making all the patterns in this book—from the pot holder, being the easiest, right up to the more intricate lacy handkerchief edgings.

I have also included a Handy Reference Guide at the back of the book.

Crochet is a satisfying, totally mind absorbing and rewarding hobby. I'm sure you will agree with me.

Sharon White

1 Right-Handed Instructions

To begin you need a 4.00 mm hook and a ball of 8 ply pure wool crepe.

Remember you are learning a new skill. It will be difficult at first, but the more you practise, the more familiar it will be to you and the easier it will become.

First pick up your hook with your right hand. There is no right or wrong way to hold the hook, although it is important to place your thumb on the flat part of the hook. Hold it the way that feels most comfortable for you. Your right hand will do most of the work. When you crochet your right hand will manoeuvre the hook around the yarn to form each stitch.

Slip Knot

You must always start with a slip knot.
Using 8 ply wool carefully follow Steps 1 to 4.

Step 1
Form a loop with the little end of the wool on top.

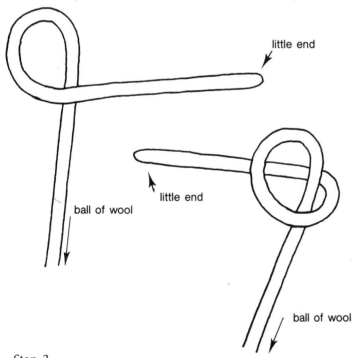

Step 2
Pass the little end under the loop.

Step 3
Using your hook, from front to back, slip hook under the little end and pull towards you. With your left hand grasp both ends of the wool.

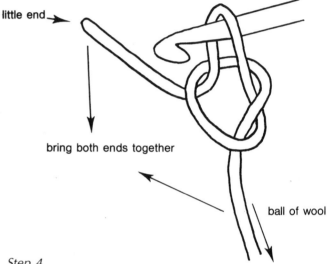

Step 4
Your slip knot is correct if the little end can be pulled to tighten the loop.

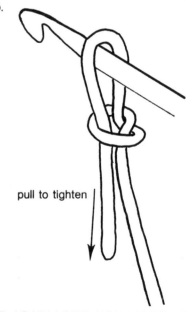

TRY AGAIN AND AGAIN UNTIL YOU MASTER THE SLIP KNOT.

Holding the Yarn

Your right hand holds the hook. Your left hand holds the yarn, in such a way that it controls the tension of your work. Thread the wool around your fingers by following Steps 1 to 3.

Step 1

Hold left hand flat, palm down. Using right hand place yarn in between fingers 3 and 4.

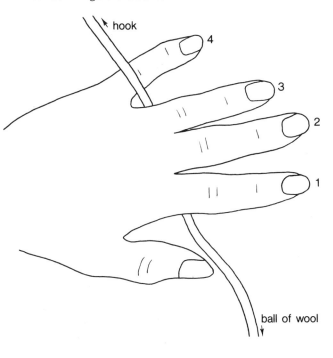

Step 3

Hold the slip knot with finger 2 and your thumb.

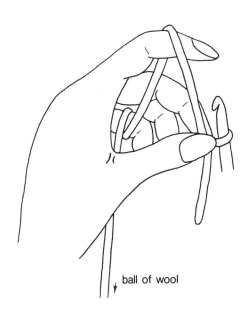

Step 2

Take yarn around finger 4, under your hand and up between fingers 1 and 2. Bring yarn over finger 1. Bend finger 4.

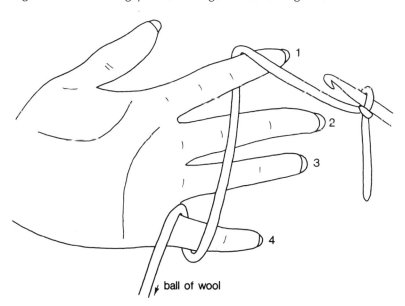

Chain Stitch (ch) ○

The foundation chain is the basis of all crochet. The symbol for chain in graph work is ○.

With your right hand move hook from left to right under yarn and draw through the loop on your hook. Now move the thumb and middle finger of your left hand to hold that first chain. This will give you better control of your work.

TRY AGAIN.

Yarn over hook, then draw through. As your right hand makes a chain, your left hand will release just enough yarn to work that stitch, then tighten again.

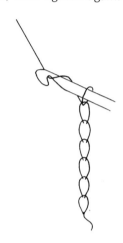

A FEW SIMPLE POINTS TO REMEMBER WHEN LEARNING TO MAKE A CHAIN STITCH

- After you have worked 2 or 3 chain stitches, bring your thumb and middle finger back to hold the work just under the hook. This gives you better control of your work.
- You must learn to release the little finger of your left hand and allow the yarn to pass freely through your fingers when a stitch is being made, then tighten again when the chain stitch is finished.
- Each chain stitch should be exactly the same size. This comes with practice.
- Count only the chain stitches you have worked. Never count the loop on the hook.

5 chain

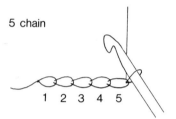

1 2 3 4 5

2 Left-Handed Instructions

To begin you need a 4.00 mm hook and a ball of 8 ply pure wool crepe.

Remember you are learning a new skill. It will be difficult at first, but the more you practise, the more familiar it will be to you and the easier it will become.

First pick up your hook with your left hand. There is no right or wrong way to hold the hook, although it is important to place your thumb on the flat part of the hook. Hold it the way it feels most comfortable for you. Your left hand will do most of the work. When you crochet your left hand will manoeuvre the hook around the yarn to form each stitch.

Slip Knot

You must always start with a slip knot.
Using 8 ply wool carefully follow Steps 1 to 4.

Step 1
Form a loop with the little end of the wool on top.

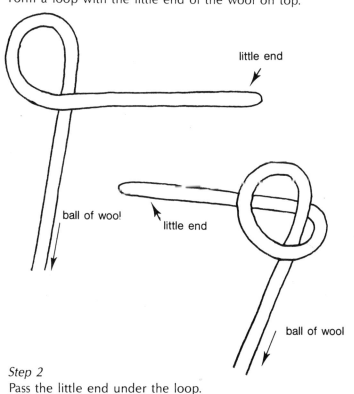

Step 2
Pass the little end under the loop.

Step 3
Using your hook, from front to back, slip hook under the little end and pull towards you. With your right hand grasp both ends of the wool.

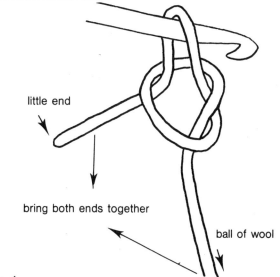

Step 4
Your slip knot is correct if the little end can be pulled to tighten the loop.

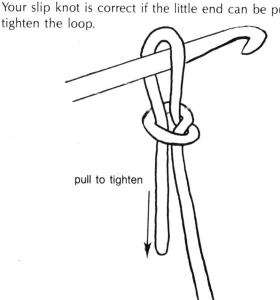

TRY AGAIN AND AGAIN UNTIL YOU MASTER THE SLIP KNOT.

Holding the Yarn

Your left hand holds the hook. Your right hand holds the yarn, in such a way that it controls the tension of your work. Thread the wool around your fingers by following Steps 1 to 3.

Step 1

Hold right hand flat, palm down. Using left hand place yarn in between fingers 3 and 4.

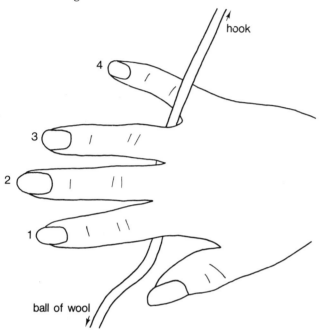

Step 2

Take yarn around finger 4, under your hand and up between fingers 1 and 2. Bring yarn over finger 1. Bend finger 4.

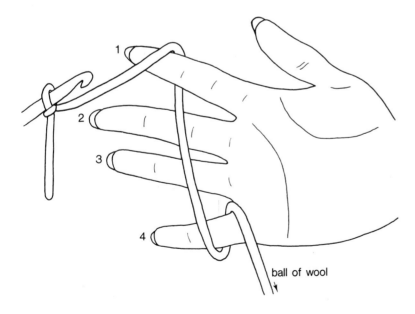

Step 3

Hold the slip knot with finger 2 and your thumb.

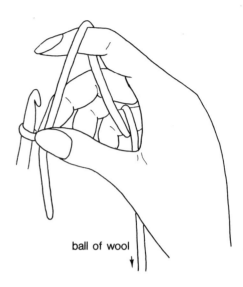

Chain Stitch (ch) ○

The foundation chain is the basis of all crochet. The symbol for chain in graph work is ○.

With your left hand move hook from right to left under yarn and draw through the loop on your hook. Now move the thumb and middle finger of your right hand to hold that first chain. This will give you better control of your work.

TRY AGAIN.

Yarn over hook, then draw through. As your left hand makes a chain, your right hand will release just enough yarn to work that stitch, then tighten again.

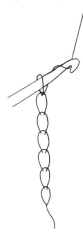

A FEW SIMPLE POINTS TO REMEMBER WHEN LEARNING TO MAKE A CHAIN STITCH

- After you have worked 2 or 3 chain stitches, bring your thumb and middle finger back to hold the work just under the hook. This gives you better control of your work.
- You must learn to release the little finger of your right hand and allow the yarn to pass freely through your fingers when a stitch is being made, then tighten again when the chain stitch is finished.
- Each chain stitch should be exactly the same size. This comes with practice.
- Count only the chain stitches you have worked. Never count the loop on the hook.

5 chain

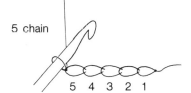

5 4 3 2 1

I'll let you in on a little secret—I am left-handed. Yes, and I have been teaching right-handed people to crochet for years. So please don't be put off just because you are left-handed.

You must read the written patterns exactly as they are written. Remember to read, comprehend, then crochet. For a left-handed beginner written patterns are easier to work from than a graph.

In graph patterns everyone reads from *right* to *left*. It is much easier for the right-handed person because they crochet from right to left.

The left-handed person must learn to read the pattern from right to left, comprehend it and then crochet it from left to right.

The results will be exactly the same for both left-handed and right-handed crocheters.

The instructions in this book are written for right-handed persons, as they are the majority. Any special instruction that affects the left-handed person I have put in brackets.

A photograph of left-handed crab stitch appears on page 22.

3 Double Crochet (dc) +

+ is the symbol for double crochet in graph work. Double crochet is used in almost every pattern you follow. You must learn this one very well.

Using 4.00 mm hook and 8 ply pure wool carefully follow Step 1 through to Step 5.

Step 1
Make 11 foundation chain.

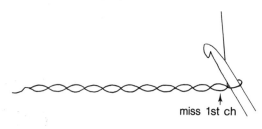

miss 1st ch

Step 2
Miss first chain, hook into top loop of next chain, yarn over hook and draw through (you should have 2 loops on hook), yarn over hook and draw through remaining 2 loops on hook.

YOU HAVE JUST WORKED ONE DOUBLE CROCHET (dc)

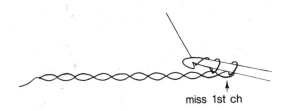

miss 1st ch

Step 3
*Hook into next ch, yarn over hook and draw through, yarn over hook and draw through remaining 2 loops on hook *; repeat from * to * in each chain to end.

YOU SHOULD FINISH UP WITH 10 dc.

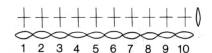

Step 4
Make 1 chain, turn your work.
Hook into the first dc from front to back under the top 2 threads that form the ridge, yarn over hook and draw through, yarn over hook and draw through remaining 2 loops on hook.

Step 5
* Hook into next dc under top ridge, yarn over hook and draw through, yarn over hook and draw through remaining 2 loops on hook.*
Repeat from * to * in each double crochet to end.

YOU SHOULD STILL HAVE 10 dc.

Repeat Steps 4 and 5 until you are quite confident you know this stitch well.

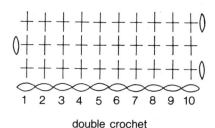

double crochet

Please Note: The correct way to work your first row of dc is to go into 2 loops of each foundation chain to end. This is much harder to do. If you find it too difficult, go back to working your first row through 1 loop only. There is very little difference to the look of the work.

The simple Pot Holder pattern on page 15 uses double crochet throughout. It is a good way to practise your double crochet.

> TIP: When you turn your work the yarn should be at the back of the work ready to begin the next stitch.
>
> If your yarn is at the front of your work, turn back and turn your work the opposite way. Now your yarn is at the back.

Pot holder, page 15

Cushion, page 18

Face washer edgings, page 29

Face washer and handtowel set, page 30

4 Pot Holder

Materials
  4.00 mm hook
  1 50 g ball 8 ply pure wool (main colour)
  small quantity 8 ply pure wool (contrast colour)
  2 small safety pins

Measurements: 15 cm (6'') square

Basic Square
Using 4.00 mm hook and main colour work 32 ch.

Row 1: Miss 1st ch, 1 dc in each ch to end. (31 dc)

This is the front of your work. Put a safety pin in the middle of this row. It will help you to recognise the front of your work.

> TIP: The front of the first row of your crochet is always the front of your work unless stated otherwise.

Row 2: 1 ch, turn, 1 dc in each dc to end. (31 dc)

* Repeat Row 2 thirty times. You have now worked 32 rows in all.
Fasten off by cutting yarn 15 cm (6'') from hook, yarn over hook and draw yarn right through. Gently tighten the loop.

Edging
Begin by working a slip knot with contrast colour and placing loop on hook.
With front of work facing and using 4.00 mm hook, work 1 dc in top right corner of square—2 stitches across and 2 rows down (left-handers work 1 dc in top left corner of square) Put a safety pin in top 2 threads of this dc. This will help you find the 1st dc at the end of the round.

> TIP: Edging is worked over 2 rows of double crochet.

Round 1: * 1 ch, miss 1 dc, 1 dc in next dc *; rep from * to * 12 times, 1 ch, miss 1 dc, (1 dc, 1 ch, 1 dc, 1 ch, 1 dc) in corner dc, * 1 ch, miss 1 row, 1 dc in next row *;

rep from * to * 12 times, 1 ch, miss 1 row, (1 dc, 1 ch, 1 dc, 1 ch, 1 dc) in corner dc, * 1 ch, miss 1 dc, 1 dc in next dc *; rep from * to * 12 times, 1 ch, miss 1 dc (1 dc, 1 ch, 1 dc, 1 ch, 1 dc) in corner dc, * 1 ch, miss 1 row, 1 dc in next row *; rep from * to * 12 times, 1 ch, miss 1 row, (1 dc, 1 ch, 1 dc, 1 ch) in corner dc, 1 sl st in 1st dc (where safety pin is).

> TIP: sl st means slip stitch—hook into 1st dc, yarn over hook and draw through dc and loop on hook (joining stitch).

Fasten off.
Darn in all loose ends on the wrong side.
Gently press pot holder on the wrong side.

Optional Attach metal ring to corner of pot holder if desired.

5 Treble (tr) †

† is the symbol for treble in graph work. Treble is the most popular stitch of all. In fact, most patterns are a variation of treble.

Again, you must learn this one well.

Using 4.00 mm hook and 8 ply pure wool carefully follow Step 1 through to Step 6.

Step 1
Make 12 foundation chain.

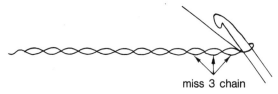

miss 3 chain

Step 2
Miss first 3 chain, yarn over hook, hook into top loop of next ch, yarn over hook and draw through (you should have 3 equal sized loops on hook), yarn over hook and draw through first 2 loops on hook, yarn over hook and draw through remaining 2 loops on hook.

YOU HAVE JUST WORKED ONE TREBLE (tr).

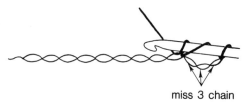

miss 3 chain

Step 3
* Yarn over hook, hook in next ch, yarn over hook and draw through, yarn over hook and draw through first 2 loops on hook, yarn over hook and draw through remaining 2 loops on hook *; repeat from * to * in each chain to end.

YOU SHOULD FINISH UP WITH 10 tr.

You must count the first 3 ch as the first treble.

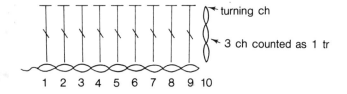

turning ch

3 ch counted as 1 tr

1 2 3 4 5 6 7 8 9 10

Step 4
Make 3 chain, turn your work. This 3 ch becomes the first treble of this row. The 3rd ch is called the 'turning chain'. You must remember that the turning ch is the last stitch on the next row. It is often helpful to put a small safety pin under top 2 loops of this 3rd ch just after you have worked it. This will help you to find the last stitch at the end of the next row.

Step 5
Miss 1st tr, yarn over hook, hook into next tr from front to back under the top 2 threads that form the ridge, yarn over hook and draw through. You should have 3 equal sized loops on hook. Yarn over hook and draw through first 2 loops on hook, yarn over hook and draw through the remaining 2 loops on hook.

THIS IS THE SECOND TREBLE—THE FIRST 3 ch BECAME THE FIRST TREBLE.

Step 6
* Yarn over hook, hook in next tr under top ridge, yarn over hook and draw through, yarn over hook and draw through first 2 loops, yarn over hook and draw through the remaining 2 loops on hook. *
Repeat from * to * in each tr to end.
Make sure you work the last tr into the top of the turning ch (always under 2 loops of ch).

YOU SHOULD STILL HAVE 10 tr.

Repeat Steps 4 to 6 inclusive until you know this stitch well.

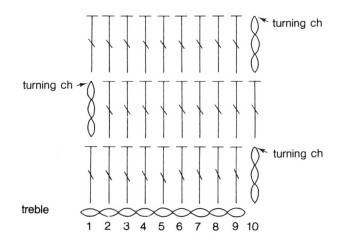

turning ch

turning ch

turning ch

treble

1 2 3 4 5 6 7 8 9 10

16

Another method of turning on a treble row
Work Steps 1 to 3 inclusive from page 16.

Step 4
Turn your work.
(1 dc, 1 ch) in first treble.
This now becomes the first treble of this row. It looks more like a treble than 3 chain and is often preferable to 3 chain at the beginning of a row.

Step 5
Yarn over hook, hook into next tr from front to back under top 2 threads that form the ridge, yarn over hook and draw through. You should have 3 equal sized loops on hook. Yarn over hook and draw through first 2 loops on hook, yarn over hook and draw through the remaining 2 loops on hook.

THIS IS THE SECOND TREBLE—THE FIRST (1 dc, 1 ch) BECAME THE FIRST TREBLE.

Step 6
* Yarn over hook, hook in next tr under top ridge, yarn over hook and draw through; yarn over hook and draw through first 2 loops, yarn over hook and draw through the remaining 2 loops on hook. *
Repeat from * to * in each tr to end.
Make sure you work the last tr into the top of the turning ch (always under 2 loops of ch).

YOU SHOULD STILL HAVE 10 tr.

Repeat Steps 4 to 6 inclusive until you feel confident you are making each tr exactly the same.

You must learn both ways of turning. 3 ch at the beginning of a row is more useful in doilies and when working rounds.

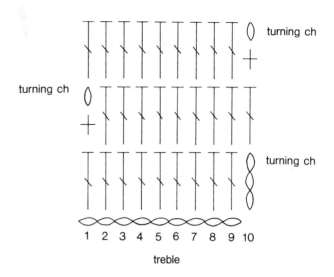

(1 dc, 1 ch) at the beginning of a row is most often used in garments or where a straight edge is required. When working (1 dc, 1 ch), the 1 ch is called the 'turning chain'. Don't forget to put a small safety pin through 2 threads of the 1 ch as soon as you have worked it, as this helps you to find the last stitch on your next row.

Please Note: The correct way to work your first row of tr is to go into 2 loops of each foundation chain to end. This is much harder to do. If you find it too difficult, go back to working your first row through 1 loop only. There is very little difference to the look of the work.

Turn the page to the Cushion pattern, which is designed to help you practise your trebles.

6 Cushion

I have chosen to work this cushion in acrylic. Acrylic is a little more difficult to crochet than wool—however, it is even more difficult to crochet in fluffy acrylic. I will let you decide which one is most suitable for you.

Materials
- 4.00 mm hook
- 150 g 8 ply acrylic
- 2 small safety pins
- 35 × 35 cm cushion insert

Measurements: 35 cm (14″) square

Square (make 2)
Using 4.00 mm hook and 8 ply acrylic make 4 ch. Join with 1 sl st into the 1st of the 4 ch to form a ring.

Round 1: 3 ch, 2 tr into centre ring, (1 ch, 3 tr into same centre ring) 3 times, 1 ch, 1 sl st in top of turning ch (you should have four groups of 3 tr and four 1 ch spaces).

> TIP: This is the front of your work. Place a safety pin into the front of this round to help you recognise the *right side*.

Round 2: 3 ch, (put a safety pin in top 2 threads of 3rd ch to help you find the top of the turning chain at the end of the round). TURN, 2 tr in 1 ch sp directly below 3 ch, 1 ch, 3 tr into same 1 ch sp (corner made), * 1 ch, (3 tr, 1 ch, 3 tr) in next 1 ch sp *; repeat from * to * twice, 1 ch, 1 sl st in top of turning ch (where the safety pin is). (4 corners made.)

> TIP: This is the back of your work—the *wrong side*.

Round 3: 3 ch, TURN, 2 tr in 1 ch sp directly below 3 ch, * 1 ch, (3 tr, 1 ch, 3 tr) in next 1 ch sp, 1 ch, 3 tr in next 1 ch sp*; repeat from * to * twice, 1 ch, (3 tr, 1 ch, 3 tr) in next 1 ch sp, 1 ch, 1 sl st in top of turning ch.

Round 4: 3 ch, TURN, 2 tr in 1 ch sp directly below 3 ch, *1 ch, (3 tr, 1 ch, 3 tr) in next 1 ch sp, (1 ch, 3 tr in next 1 ch sp) twice *; rep from * to * twice, 1 ch, (3 tr, 1 ch, 3 tr) in next 1 ch sp, 1 ch, 3 tr in next 1 ch sp, 1 ch, 1 sl st in top of turning ch.

Round 5: 3 ch, TURN, 2 tr in 1 ch sp directly below 3 ch, 1 ch, 3 tr in next 1 ch sp, * 1 ch, (3 tr, 1 ch, 3 tr) in next 1 ch sp, (1 ch, 3 tr in next 1 ch sp) 3 times *; rep from * to * twice, 1 ch, (3 tr, 1 ch, 3 tr) in next 1 ch sp, 1 ch, 3 tr in next 1 ch sp, 1 ch, 1 sl st in top of turning ch.

Round 6: 3 ch, TURN, 2 tr in 1 ch sp directly below 3 ch, 1 ch, 3 tr in next 1 ch sp, * 1 ch, (3 tr, 1 ch, 3 tr) in next 1 ch sp, (1 ch, 3 tr in next 1 ch sp) 4 times *; rep from * to * twice, 1 ch, (3 tr, 1 ch, 3 tr) in next 1 ch sp, (1 ch, 3 tr in next 1 ch sp) twice, 1 ch, 1 sl st in top of turning ch.

Continue in this way, increasing 1 ch and 3 tr along each side of cushion until 17 rounds have been completed. (Your work should measure approximately 35 cm square.) Fasten off and darn in all loose ends.

Joining both sides together
With wrong sides together, pin the front of the cushion to the back.
With right side of cushion facing, using 4.00 mm hook and 8 ply acrylic, join yarn to third 1 ch sp from top left corner (*left-handers* join yarn to third 1 ch sp from top right corner), going through both sides together.

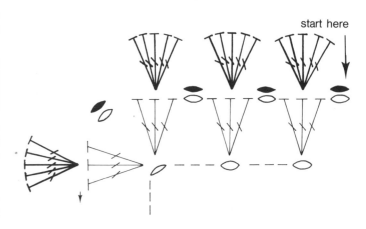

cushion edging

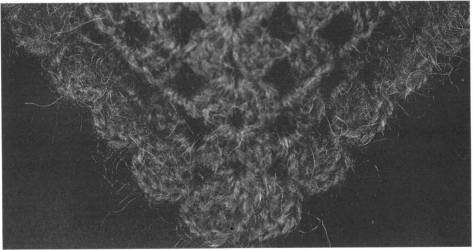

Edging

1 ch, * 5 tr in centre of next cluster (put the hook through 2nd tr of the first side and 2nd tr of the second side together), 1 sl st in next 1 ch sp through both sides together *; rep from * to * around the edge of cushion stopping at beginning of the last side; slip the cushion insert inside the cushion and continue as before to end of last side, 1 sl st in 1st ch.

Fasten off and darn in all loose ends.

7 Other Basic Stitches

Slip Stitch (sl st) ●
● is the symbol for slip stitch in graph work.
A slip stitch is a joining stitch—hook into work, yarn over hook, draw yarn through the work and the loop on hook together.

1. A slip stitch is used to join chain to form a ring,
   e.g. make 8 ch, 1 sl st in 1st ch to form a ring.

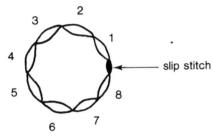

2. A slip stitch is used to finish a round,
   e.g. 1 sl st in top of turning ch.

slip stitch in top of turning ch

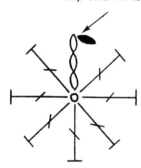

3. A slip stitch is used to move the yarn further along the row,
   e.g. sl st across first 8 tr.

slip stitch across first 8 tr

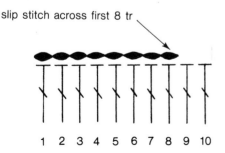

This means you must slip stitch in every tr until you reach 8th tr—the yarn is now at the right place to start the next row (often used for armhole shaping),

e.g. sl st to centre of next 5 ch loop.

slip stitch to centre of next 5 ch loop

This means you must slip stitch in every stitch until you reach the centre of next 5 ch loop—the yarn is now in the centre of the loop, ready to begin the next row.

Half Treble (htr) ⊤
⊤ is the symbol for half treble in graph work.

Try this sample:
Work 21 ch, miss 2 ch, * yarn over hook, hook into next ch, yarn over hook and draw through, yarn over hook and draw through the remaining 3 loops on hook; rep from * to end of row.

The 1st 2 ch count as the first half treble.

You should have 20 half trebles.
* Work 2 ch, turn, miss 1st htr, 1 htr in every htr to end. Don't forget to work your last htr in top of turning ch. (20 htr) *

Repeat from * to * until you have mastered the half treble.

half treble

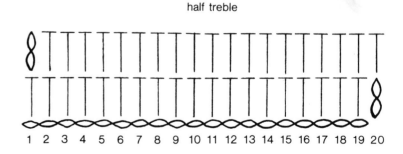

20

Double Treble (dtr)

 is the symbol for double treble in graph work.

Try this sample:

Work 23 ch, miss 4 ch, * (yarn over hook) twice, hook into next ch, yarn over hook and draw through (you should have 4 equal loops on hook), yarn over hook and draw through 1st 2 loops on hook, yarn over hook and draw through next 2 loops on hook, yarn over hook and draw through remaining 2 loops on hook; rep from * to end.

The 1st 4 ch count as the first double treble.
You should have 20 double trebles.

* Work 4 ch, turn, miss 1st dtr, 1 dtr in every dtr to end. Don't forget to work your last dtr in top of turning ch. (20 dtr) *

Repeat from * to * until you have mastered the double treble.

double treble

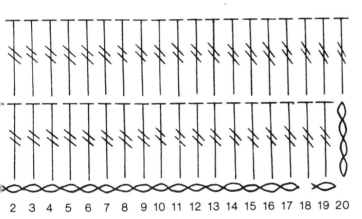

Triple Treble (ttr)

 is the symbol for triple treble in graph work.

Try this sample:

Work 24 ch, miss 5 ch, * (yarn over hook) 3 times, hook into next ch, yarn over hook and draw through (you should have 5 equal loops on hook), yarn over hook and draw through 1st 2 loops on hook, yarn over hook and draw through next 2 loops on hook, yarn over hook and draw through next 2 loops on hook, yarn over hook and draw through remaining 2 loops on hook; rep from * to end

The 1st 5 ch count as the first triple treble.
You should have 20 triple trebles.

* Work 5 ch, turn, miss 1st ttr, 1 ttr in every ttr to end. Don't forget to work your last ttr in top of turning ch. (20 ttr) *

Repeat from * to * until you have mastered the triple treble.

triple treble

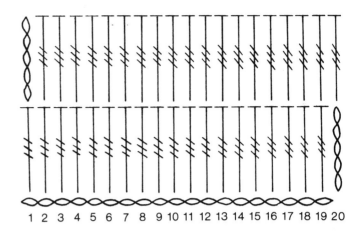

Unusual Stitches

You may occasionally come across these stitches.

Quadruple treble (quad tr) yoh 4 times, hook into work, yoh and draw through, (yoh and draw through next 2 loops on hook) 4 times, yoh and draw through rem 2 loops on hook.

Quintuple treble (quin tr) yoh 5 times, hook into work, yoh and draw through, (yoh and draw through next 2 loops on hook) 5 times, yoh and draw through rem 2 loops on hook.

Sextuple treble (sext tr) yoh 6 times, hook into work, yoh and draw through, (yoh and draw through next 2 loops on hook) 6 times, yoh and draw through rem 2 loops on hook.

Bands

A crochet garment may have knitted or crochet bands and cuffs.

Knitted Bands

After knitting the band always cast off VERY LOOSELY. Do not cut the yarn, turn and work the first row of crochet directly into the cast off edge of the knitted band. (See photograph page 22.)

Crochet Bands

Crochet bands are made by working double crochet into the BACK LOOP ONLY. (See photograph page 22.)

Try this sample:
Work 15 ch,
Row 1: miss 1st ch, 1 dc in each ch to end. (14 dc)
Row 2: 1 ch, turn, 1 dc in BACK LOOP ONLY of each dc to end. (14 dc)

Knitted band

Crochet band

Instead of inserting hook through the top 2 threads of each double crochet, insert hook down into the back loop only (from front to back) and work a double crochet as normal.

Repeat Row 2 until your band is the required length. Do not cut the yarn, turn and work the first row of crochet into the top edge of your band.

Crab Stitch

Crab stitch can also be called reversed double crochet. Both names are apt—reversed double crochet because you work double crochet backwards and crab stitch because it is such an awkward stitch to work.

Crab stitch is always worked on a foundation row of double crochet. DO NOT TURN; twist hook and from front to back insert hook under ridge of 1st dc, hook over yarn and draw down through work (you should have 2 loops on hook), yarn over hook and draw through remaining 2 loops on hook; * hook in next dc, hook over yarn and draw through, yoh and draw through rem 2 loops on hook; rep from * to end. Fasten off.

Crab stitch takes a lot of practice to achieve, but after a while it does become easier and more even. These photographs show the difference between right-handed and left-handed crab stitch.

Right-handed crab stitch

Left-handed crab stitch

8 Shaping and Finishing

Increasing

Increasing is very easy. It means working 2 stitches in only 1 stitch of your work,

e.g. 1 tr in 1st tr, *inc*, 1 tr in each tr to 2nd last tr, *inc*, 1 tr in last tr.

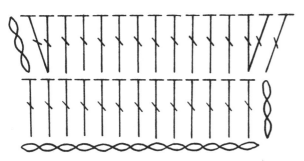

increasing

This means 1 tr in 1st tr, *2 tr in next tr*, 1 tr in each tr to 2nd last tr, *2 tr in next tr*, 1 tr in last tr.

Increasing is usually worked 1 stitch in from the edge. This keeps the edge straight and makes it easier to sew the pieces together.

Decreasing

Decreasing is a little more difficult. It means working 1 stitch only over 2 stitches of your work.

To Decrease in Treble

e.g. 1 tr in 1st tr, *dec*, 1 tr in each tr to 3rd last tr, *dec*, 1 tr in last tr.

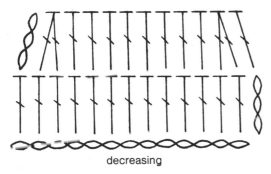

decreasing

This means 1 tr in 1st tr, *(yarn over hook, hook into next st, yarn over hook and draw through, yarn over hook and draw through 1st 2 loops on hook) twice, yarn over hook and draw through remaining 3 loops on hook; 1 tr in each tr to 3rd last tr, (yarn over hook, hook into next st, yarn over hook and draw through; yarn over hook and draw through 1st 2 loops on hook) twice, yarn over hook and draw through remaining 3 loops on hook; 1 tr in last tr.*

To Decrease in Double Crochet

e.g. 1 dc in 1st dc, *dec*, 1 dc in each dc to last 3 dc, *dec*, 1 dc in last dc.

decreasing

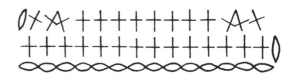

This means 1 dc in 1st dc, *(hook into next dc, yarn over hook and draw through) twice, yarn over hook and draw through remaining 3 loops on hook; 1 dc in each dc to last 3 dc, (hook in next dc, yarn over hook and draw through) twice, yarn over hook and draw through remaining 3 loops on hook; 1 dc in last dc.*

Decreasing is usually worked 1 stitch in from the edge. This keeps the edge straight and makes it easier to sew the pieces together.

In some patterns a decrease is made by simply missing one stitch.

Front of Work

The front of the first row of crochet is always the front of the work unless stated otherwise.

To Fasten Off

Fasten off by cutting yarn 15 cm (6'') from hook, yarn over hook and draw yarn right through. Gently tighten the loop. Always sew seams together before darning in all loose ends.

Joining New Yarn

Joining a New Ball

Always try to join the yarn at the edge of your work. Don't feel you are wasting the leftover yarn—you can use that for sewing up seams.

Joining in a new ball

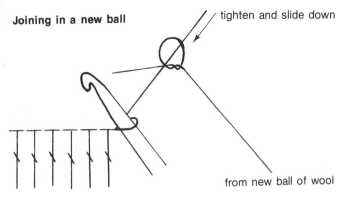

tighten and slide down

from new ball of wool

I find this method the most satisfactory: Cut the yarn from the old ball approximately 15 cm (6'') away from the hook. With new ball, make half a knot with loose end and slip over the old yarn, tighten knot and slide yarn down to hook; now you are ready to continue your crochet.

If you must join the yarn in the middle of the row, choose a place where it won't be noticeable, e.g. in a cluster of treble in preference to a 5 ch loop.

Joining Yarn to an Edge
There are three ways of attaching the yarn to an edge:

1. Hook into edging, yarn over hook and draw yarn right through, tie a firm knot at the top of the edge, hook back into same sp, yarn over hook and draw through edging, work 1 ch, then begin.

2. Make a slip knot and place loop on hook, insert hook into edging, then begin.

3. Hook into edging, yarn over hook and draw through edging and work 1 ch, then begin.

It is preferable not to use knots in your work. As you are learning, start with No. 1 which is the easiest, then progress to No. 2 and then to No. 3.

Buttonholes
Row 1: 1 ch, 1 dc to end, turn.
Mark position of buttonholes with pins.
Row 2: 1 ch, * 1 dc in each dc to pin, 3 ch, miss 3 dc, rep from * to end, turn.
Row 3: 1 ch, * 1 dc in each dc to buttonhole, 3 dc into buttonhole, rep from * to end.

Use 2 ch buttonholes for smaller buttons and 4 ch buttonholes for larger buttons.

Button Loops
Mark position of button loops with pins.
Row 1: * 1 sl st in each st along edge to pin, 3 ch, miss 2 sts, rep from * to end.

Buttonholes

Button loops

24

Sewing Seams

Joining Top Edges Together

Pin right sides together. This seam is worked on the WRONG side. Use the same yarn as used for crochet and a blunt sewing needle.

Using a whipped seam weave needle from back to front under the top ridge of corresponding stitches. Do not sew tightly. The seam should have as much give as your work. After you have joined the seams you can darn in all loose threads.

Joining Side Edges Together

Pin wrong sides together. This seam is worked on the RIGHT side. Use the same yarn as used for crochet and a blunt sewing needle.

Using a flat seam weave needle through 2 threads on one side of work and then straight across and weave through 2 threads on the other side. Do not sew too tight. The seam should have as much give as the rest of your work. The two sides should sit flat and just come together.

After you have joined the seams you can darn in all loose ends.

Joining top edges together

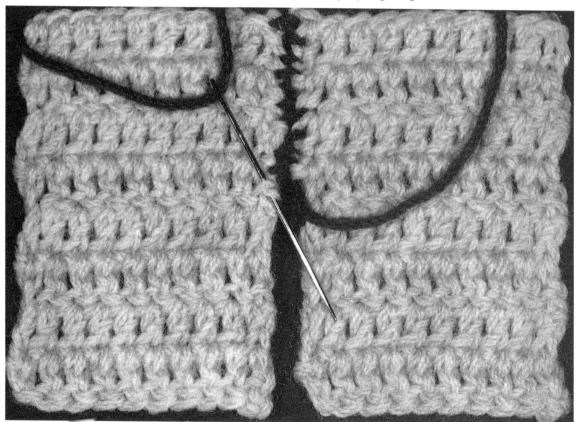

Joining side edges together

9 How to Read a Pattern

During my years of teaching crochet I was frequently told, 'I can crochet, but I can't read a pattern'. It seems to be a common problem. Once you understand the following rules it should all just fall into place.

Rule No. 1: Check your tension
Rule No. 2: Read from comma to comma
Rule No. 3: Brackets
Rule No. 4: (   ) 3 times
Rule No. 5: Repeat from * to *
Rule No. 6: Learn your abbreviations
Rule No. 7: Use the correct materials
Rule No. 8: Choose a good quality pattern

Reading a crochet pattern is quite easy once you have mastered these rules.
Also, try working the patterns in this book, starting from the Pot Holder, which is the easiest, and work up to the Handkerchief Edges, the most intricate.
Try learning the graph symbols as well.
All the patterns in this book have been designed with one thing in mind—to teach you to read a pattern successfully.

Rule No. 1: Check Your Tension

Correct tension is important for you to achieve perfect results,

e.g. TENSION: 18 tr and 10 rows to 10 cm using 4.00 mm hook and 8 ply pure wool.

This means the designer of the pattern has used a tension of 18 tr to 10 cm and 10 rows of treble to 10 cm, using a 4.00 mm hook and 8 ply pure wool. For you to crochet that pattern and have it turn out the same as the original, you must have a similar tension. This will require your making a sample piece of work.
When you make your sample piece, always work more stitches and rows than required,

e.g.   Work 30 ch,
       Miss 1st 3 ch, 1 tr in each ch to end, (28 tr)
       Work a further 11 rows treble,
       Fasten off.

Measure your work as illustrated below.

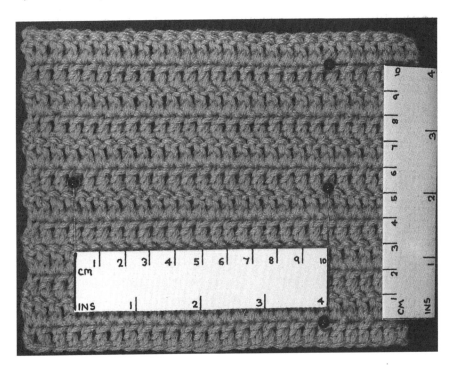

If you have more than 18 tr and more than 10 rows to 10 cm, work the sample again, using a hook one size larger.

If you have less than 18 tr and less than 10 rows to 10 cm, work the sample again using a hook one size smaller.

Once you have achieved a tension similar to the one required, you are ready to start the pattern.

Rule No. 2: Read from Comma to Comma
In my opinion this is the most important rule of all. When you read a crochet pattern you must read from comma to comma,

e.g. 1 dc in next ch, miss 2 ch, 1 tr in next ch,
Read to 1st comma, work it, read to 2nd comma, comprehend it, read to 3rd comma, work it.

Rule No. 3: Brackets
The commas within the brackets do not apply to Rule No. 2. Whatever is written inside the brackets is read as one instruction,

e.g. 1 dc in same sp, into next sp work (2 tr, 2 ch, 2 tr),
Read to 1st comma, work it, read to 2nd comma as follows: into next space work (something).

Once you have understood that you have to work (something) into the next space, you go inside the brackets to find out WHAT you work into the next space. You must work 2 tr, 2 ch, 2 tr ALL into the next space.

Another way of writing the same instruction would be:
    1 dc in same sp, (2 tr, 2 ch, 2 tr) into next sp,

Square or large brackets take preference over small or rounded brackets,
e.g. [1 dc in next sp, (2 tr, 2 ch, 2 tr) into next sp] twice,

You would first read the instruction as [   ] twice, then say, 'What do I work twice?' You work [1 dc in next sp, (2 tr, 2 ch, 2 tr) in next sp] once and then [1 dc in next sp, (2 tr, 2 ch, 2 tr) in next sp] again.

Rule No. 4: (   ) 3 times
When an instruction states (   ) 3 times, it means you must read the brackets three times in all,

e.g. 1 tr in next sp, (6 tr in next sp) 3 times,
Read to 1st comma, work it, read to 2nd comma as follows: 6 tr in next space, 6 tr in next space, 6 tr in next space.

To save writing the same instruction out three times in a row it is placed in brackets.

e.g. 1 tr in next sp, (1 tr, 1 ch) 2 times and 1 tr into next sp,
Read to 1st comma, work it, read to 2nd comma as follows: 1 tr, 1 ch, 1 tr, 1 ch, 1 tr ALL have to be worked into the next space.

Rule No. 5: Rep from * to *
This rule is quite different to Rule No. 4,

e.g. * 1 dc in next sp, miss 1 sp, 6 tr in next sp *, rep from * to * 2 times,
*Read to 1st comma, work it, read to 2nd comma, comprehend it, read to 3rd comma, work it, read to 4th comma, work it as follows: * 1 dc in next sp, miss 1 sp, 6 tr in next sp *, once and then * 1 dc in next sp, miss 1 sp, 6 tr in next sp *, again.*

*** are often used to mark certain parts of a pattern which are later repeated,

e.g. Work the same as for Lemon Washer to end of Round 2. ***

This saves writing the same instructions out again by telling you to work the same instructions as for the Lemon Washer but stopping when you see ***

Rule No. 6: Learn Your Abbreviations
It makes pattern reading so much easier when you know the abbreviations. To learn your abbreviations, turn to Chapter 15—Handy Reference Guide.

Rule No. 7: Use the Correct Materials
Always use the correct size hook and ply wool as indicated in your pattern (except in achieving the right tension). If you use different materials you may have poor results.

Rule No. 8: Choose a Good Quality Pattern
Especially if you are a beginner, choose a pattern from a well known company, e.g. Patons, Milford. The Australian Wool Corporation publishes excellent crochet books. A word of caution about some of the patterns printed in women's magazines— in my experience they often leave out important commas, or even words, which makes working out the pattern similar to solving a crossword puzzle.

Graph Work
You need to know how to read a pattern written in words as most of our patterns have been written that way.

You need to know how to read a pattern written in graph as this is how more patterns are going to be written. The advantage of a graph pattern is that it can be read by people from every country. The symbols are the same world-wide.

Try to become familiar with both ways of reading a crochet pattern, i.e. patterns written in words and patterns written in graph.

Chapter 14—Handkerchief Edgings, includes both written and graph patterns for each edge.

First, crochet the edge reading from the written pattern. Then try working the same edge again reading from the graph pattern. Remember you must read the graph from RIGHT to LEFT. The number in the circle indicates the round number, e.g. ②means the beginning of Round 2. Your work should look similar to the graph pattern.

(LEFT-HANDERS—please remember that although you read the graph from RIGHT to LEFT, you actually crochet from left to right. The end result will be exactly the same.)

American Patterns

Reading an American pattern can be confusing as their written abbreviations are quite different to ours.

e.g. *American* | | *Australian*
Abbreviations		*Abbreviations*
sc	is equal to our	dc
hdc	is equal to our	htr
dc	is equal to our	tr
tr	is equal to our	dtr
dtr	is equal to our	ttr
skip	is equal to our	miss
yo	is equal to our	yoh
bind off	is equal to our	cast off

American patterns refer to their yarn in a different way to us.

e.g. *American* | | *Australian*
Yarn		*Yarn*
fingering	is equal to our	4 ply
sport	is equal to our	8 ply
bulky	is equal to our	12 ply

Crochet Hooks

The following chart will help you to convert the old hook sizes to the new metric size.

New Metric	Old Steel (cotton)	Old Aluminium (wool)
.60 mm	6	
.75 mm	5	
1.00 mm	4	
1.25 mm	3	
1.50 mm	2½	
1.75 mm	2	
2.00 mm	1	14
2.50 mm		12
3.00 mm		11
3.50 mm		9
4.00 mm		8
4.50 mm		7
5.00 mm		6
5.50 mm		5
6.00 mm		4
7.00 mm		2

10 Face Washer Edgings

Lemon Washer

This one is an old favourite. It is especially popular with those who dislike working picots.

Materials
  1.50 mm hook
  2.00 mm hook
  1 50 g ball 4 ply cotton
  1 face washer
  1 small safety pin

Note: 1 50 g ball of 4 ply cotton is sufficient to work all the edgings in this chapter.

Preparation: With front of face washer facing you, using 1.50 mm hook and 4 ply cotton, insert hook just past the corner 5 mm (⅛'') down into face washer edge. Yarn over hook, pull cotton through face washer and tie a firm knot at the edge of the washer. Hook back into the same hole in the washer, yarn over hook, pull yarn through washer and work 1 ch. This is now called your first double crochet for this pattern. Put a safety pin through two threads of your ch. This will help you find the first dc at the end of the round.

NOW YOU ARE READY TO BEGIN

> TIP: Try and keep your dc FIRM and the space between each dc EQUAL.

Lemon washer, mint washer and white washer

Round 1: Using 1.50 mm hook work 5 ch, 1 dc into face washer edge approximately 13 mm (½″) from the start, (your 5 ch should form an arch over the washer edge) *5 ch, 1 dc into face washer approximately 13 mm (½″) further along edge*; rep from * to * around the washer finishing with 5 ch, 1 sl st in 1st dc (through two threads where the safety pin is). **

Count the spaces. You need to finish the round with an even number of spaces.

> TIP: When you are at the last corner, about 8 cm (3″) away from the 1st dc, count your 5 ch spaces. You can then work the right number of spaces around the corner to give you an even number. The reason we start just past the corner is because it is less noticeable if you adjust your spaces around the corner.

Using 1.50 mm hook, slip stitch in each of next 2 ch.

Change to 2.00 mm hook.

Round 2: 1 ch, 1 dc in SAME loop, (not in the chain, but down into the space below). Put a safety pin through top 2 threads of this dc. * 5 ch, 1 dc in NEXT loop *; rep from * to * around washer finishing with 5 ch, 1 sl st in 1st dc of Round 2 (where the safety pin is), 1 sl st in each of next 2 ch. ***

Round 3: 1 ch, 1 dc in SAME loop, (put a safety pin under top 2 threads of this dc) * into NEXT loop work (2 tr, 3 ch, 2 tr, 3 ch, 2 tr), 1 dc in NEXT loop *; rep from * to * around washer ending with 1 sl st in 1st dc of Round 3 (where the safety pin is).

> TIP: Before cutting the cotton, go back over your work to check it is correct.

Fasten off.

Darn in all loose ends.
Gently press edge on wrong side.

Mint Washer

Materials: same as for Lemon Washer.
Instructions: same as for Lemon Washer right up to end of Round 1. ** For this edging you do not need to have an even number of spaces. This pattern will work out with any number of spaces.
Using 1.50 mm hook slip stitch in next 1 ch.

Change to 2.00 mm hook.

Round 2: 3 ch, (put a safety pin in top of 3rd ch through 2 threads) 2 tr in SAME space, (not in the chain, but down into the space below) * 3 ch, 3 tr in NEXT loop *; rep from * to * around washer finishing with 3 ch, 1 sl st in top of turning ch (where the safety pin is).

> TIP: Picot of 3 ch means *work 3 ch, 1 dc back into the first of the 3 ch under 2 threads.*

Round 3: sl st to centre of next 3 ch loop, (this means you have to slip stitch into every stitch until you reach the centre of the loop, i.e. 1 sl st in each of next 2 tr and 1 ch) 1 ch, 1 dc in SAME loop, (put a safety pin through the top 2 threads of this dc) * 1 ch, picot of 3 ch, 1 ch, 1 dc in NEXT loop *; rep from * to * around washer finishing with 1 sl st in 1st dc of Round 3 (where the safety pin is).
Fasten off.
Darn in all loose ends.
Gently press on wrong side.

White Washer
Materials: same as for Lemon Washer.
Instructions: same as for Lemon Washer right up to end of Round 2. ***

> TIP: Picot of 4 ch means *work 4 ch, 1 dc back into the first of the 4 ch under 2 threads.*

Round 3: 1 ch, 1 dc in SAME loop, (put a safety pin under top 2 threads of this dc) * 1 ch, into NEXT loop work (3 tr, picot of 4 ch, 3 tr), 1 ch, 1 dc in NEXT loop *; rep from * to * around washer finishing with 1 sl st in 1st dc of Round 3 (where the safety pin is).
Fasten off.
Darn in all loose ends.
Gently press on wrong side.

Apricot Face Washer and Handtowel Set

Materials
   1.50 mm hook
   2.00 mm hook
   1 50 g ball 4 ply cotton
   1 handtowel
   1 face washer
   2 small safety pins

Face Washer

Instructions: same as for Lemon Washer right up to end of Round 2. ***

> TIP: Picot of 2 ch means *work 2 ch, 1 dc back into the first of the 2 ch under 2 threads.*

Tawny tea cosy, page 35

Kitchen handtowel, page 37

Lavender bag, page 39

Handkerchief edgings, page 40

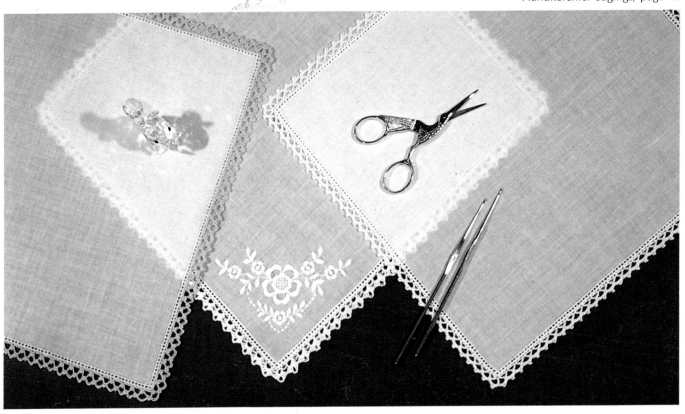

Round 3: 1 ch, 1 dc in SAME loop, (put a safety pin under top 2 threads of this dc) * 2 ch, into NEXT loop work (1 tr, picot of 2 ch, 1 tr, picot of 2 ch, 1 tr, picot of 2 ch, 1 tr), 2 ch, 1 dc in NEXT loop *; rep from * to * finishing with 1 sl st in 1st dc of Round 3 (where the safety pin is). Fasten off.

Handtowel
Worked along the lower edges of the handtowel.

Preparation: With front of handtowel facing you, using 1.50 mm hook and 4 ply cotton, insert hook into the corner of the towel 5 mm (⅛'') down. Yarn over hook, pull cotton through handtowel and tie a firm knot at the edge of the towel. Hook back into the same hole in the towel, yarn over hook, pull yarn through towel and work 1 ch. This is called your 1st dc. Put a safety pin through 2 threads of your chain. This will help you find the last dc at the end of the next row.

NOW YOU ARE READY TO BEGIN.

Don't forget—keep those dc FIRM and the space between each dc EQUAL.

Row 1: Using 1.50 mm hook work 5 ch, 1 dc into handtowel edge approx. 13 mm (½'') from the start, *5 ch, 1 dc in handtowel approximately 13 mm (½'') further along edge *; rep from * to * along the lower edge of handtowel, finishing with 1 dc right in the corner on the other side of the towel. Count the spaces. You must finish with an even number of spaces. TURN.

Change to 2.00 mm hook.

Row 2: 5 ch, (put a safety pin in top of 3rd ch. This will help you find the top of the tr at the end of the next row— the 5 ch is equivalent to '1 tr, 2 ch') * 1 dc in NEXT loop, 5 ch *; rep from * to * along edge finishing with 1 dc in last loop, 2 ch, 1 tr in 1st dc of Row 1 (where the safety pin is). 1 ch, TURN.

Row 3: 1 dc in 1st tr, * 2 ch, into next 5 ch loop work (1 tr, picot of 2 ch, 1 tr, picot of 2 ch, 1 tr, picot of 2 ch, 1 tr), 2 ch, 1 dc in NEXT loop *; rep from * to * along edge finishing with (1 tr, picot of 2 ch, 1 tr, picot of 2 ch, 1 tr, picot of 2 ch, 1 tr) in last 5 ch loop, 2 ch, 1 dc in last tr (where the safety pin is. Remember, 3 ch is equivalent to 1 tr).
Fasten off.
Repeat the edge along the other side of the handtowel.
Darn in all loose ends.
Gently press edges on the wrong side.

Apricot face washer and handtowel set

H E L P ! ! !

Do your edges resemble these photographs?

If your work looks like the top picture you are a *tight* crocheter. You need to use a hook one size larger (i.e. 2.50 mm) for the main part of the edging to rectify the problem.

If your work looks like the bottom picture you are a *loose* crocheter. You need to use a hook one size smaller (i.e. 1.75 mm) for the main part of the edging to rectify the problem.

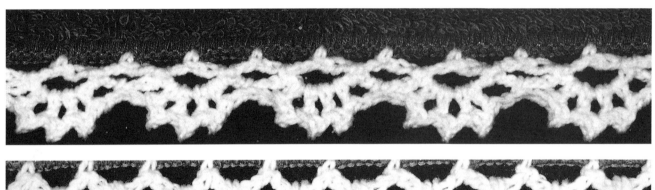

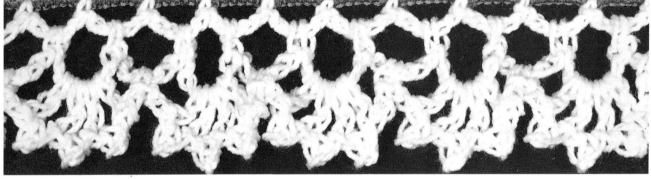

11 Tawny Tea Cosy

The idea for this design came from two young Tawny Frogmouths that I hand reared.

Materials
- 5.00 mm hook
- 5.50 mm hook
- 100 g brown/black fleck 8 ply pure wool
- 50 g white 7 ply mohair
- 25 g black 8 ply pure wool
- 4 owl eyes (available from craft shops)
- 2 owl noses (available from craft shops)

This tea cosy will fit most 4 cup teapots.

Tension: 15 tr and 8 rows to 10 cm over tr fabric using 5.50 mm hook and 1 strand of 8 ply wool (as in Inside Lining).

Eye Piece (make 4)
Using 5.50 mm hook and brown/black fleck wool and white mohair TOGETHER, work 4 ch, 1 sl st back into the 1st of the 4 ch to form a ring.

Row 1: 4 ch, (this is equivalent to 1 tr, 1 ch); (1 tr into ring, 1 ch) 11 times; 1 sl st in top of 3rd ch. (twelve tr and twelve 1 ch spaces)

Row 2: 1 sl st in 1st 1 ch sp, 3 ch, 1 tr in SAME sp, (1 ch, 2 tr in NEXT sp) 3 times, 2 tr in each 1 ch sp to end, 1 sl st in top of 3rd ch. (twelve groups of 2 tr and three 1 ch spaces).

Fasten off.

> TIP: Bobble means *[yarn over hook, hook into sp, yarn over hook and draw yarn up to a height of 2 cm (¾")]* 3 times, yarn over hook and draw through all 7 loops on hook, 1 ch to fasten.

Body (make 2)
You need two eye pieces. Use 5.50 mm hook and brown/black fleck wool and white mohair TOGETHER.

Row 1: With front of 1st eye piece facing you, join yarn to 1st 1 ch sp, 3 ch, (bobble, 1 extra ch, bobble) in SAME sp, (1 extra ch, bobble, 1 extra ch, bobble in NEXT 1 ch sp) twice; pick up second eye piece; with front of second eye piece facing you, work (1 extra ch, bobble, 1 extra ch, bobble) in each of the three 1 ch spaces, 1 tr in last 1 ch sp beside bobble. (twelve bobbles, eleven 1 ch spaces and 1 tr at each end). TURN.

Row 2: 3 ch, (bobble into top of next bobble under 2 threads, 1 extra ch) 11 times, bobble in last bobble, 1 tr in top of 3rd ch. (12 bobbles, eleven 1 ch spaces and 1 tr at each end); TURN.

Repeat Row 2 a further 6 times.

Fasten off.

Black Stripe Between Eyes (make 2)
Using 5.50 mm hook and 2 strands of black 8 ply wool, join yarn to middle of eye pieces (in 2nd tr above body through both sides of the eye pieces together), work 1 ch, 1 dc in each of next 5 tr.

Fasten off.
Attach eyes and nose.
Darn in all ends.

Inside Lining (make 2)
Using 1 strand of brown/black fleck wool *only* and 5.50 mm hook work 37 ch.

Row 1: miss 3 ch, 1 tr in each ch to end. (35 tr). TURN.

Row 2: (1 dc, 1 ch) in 1st tr, 1 tr in each tr to end (don't forget—last tr goes in top of turning ch), TURN.

Repeat Row 2 four times (35 tr).

> TIP: dec means decrease: *(yarn over hook, hook into next tr, yarn over hook and draw through, yarn over hook and draw through 2 threads only) twice; yarn over hook and draw through the remaining 3 loops. The decrease is worked over 2 trebles.*

Row 7: (1 dc, 1 ch) in 1st tr, dec, 1 tr in each tr to last 3 tr, dec, 1 tr in top of turning ch. (33 tr). TURN.

Repeat Row 7 twice. (29 tr)

Row 10: (1 dc, 1 ch) in 1st tr, 1 tr in next tr, * dec, 1 tr in next tr *; rep from * to * to the end. (20 tr).

Row 11: (1 dc, 1 ch) in 1st tr, dec, 1 tr in each tr to last 3 tr, dec, 1 tr in top of turning ch. (18 tr).

Row 12: same as Row 11. (16 tr).

Row 13: (1 dc, 1 ch) in 1st tr, 1 tr in each tr to end. (16 tr).

Row 14: same as Row 13.

Fasten off.
Darn in all loose ends.

Black Edging

Side 1:
Pin body to inside lining with wrong sides together. With front side of body facing, using 5.00 mm hook and 1 strand of black 8 ply wool, join yarn to body just below eye piece (through both sides together).

Round 1: 1 ch, 1 dc evenly along side edge (through both sides together), 3 dc in corner, 33 dc evenly along bottom edge (through both sides together), 3 dc in corner, 1 dc evenly along side edge and around head (through both sides together); 1 sl st in 1st dc of Round 1. ***

Round 2: 1 ch, 1 dc in each dc along side edge, 3 dc in corner dc, 1 dc in each dc along bottom edge, 3 dc in corner dc, 1 dc in each dc along side edge finishing just below eye piece (do not work around head section).
Fasten off.

Side 2
Same as for Side 1 to end of Round 1. ***

Round 2: 1 ch, 1 dc in each dc along side edge, in corner dc work (2 dc, 1 sl st in corner of Side 1, 1 dc), 1 dc in each dc along bottom edge, in corner dc work (1 dc, 1 sl st in corner of Side 1, 2 dc), 1 dc in each dc along side edge finishing just below eye piece; holding Side 1 and Side 2 together, 1 dc in each dc around head section (through both sides together), 1 sl st in 1st dc of Round 2.
Fasten off.
Darn in all loose threads.
If desired, brush gently with a mohair brush for a realistic look.

12 Kitchen Handtowel

Materials
(sufficient to make two handtowels)
  1.50 mm hook
  2.00 mm hook
  1 50 g ball 4 ply cotton
  1 terry towelling teatowel
  1 ruler and 1 sharp pencil
  1 cottonwool ball (for button)
  1 small safety pin

Preparation: Cut teatowel in half and hem both upper and lower edges. (The zig-zag stitch on sewing machines is useful for this.)

Lower Edge

With front side of towel facing you, using 1.50 mm hook and 4 ply cotton, join yarn to lower edge of towel 3 mm (⅛'') from corner.

Row 1: 3 ch, 2 tr in same sp, * 1 ch, miss 13 mm (½'') along towel, 3 tr in towel (all worked in same sp) *; rep from * to * along lower edge of towel finishing with 3 tr at the end of towel, TURN.

> TIP: If you find it hard to miss 13 mm evenly, turn towel to wrong side and with pencil and ruler dot every 13 mm along towel.

Change to 2.00 mm hook.

Row 2: 4 ch, * 3 tr in next 1 ch sp, 1 ch *; rep from * to * to last 1 ch sp, 3 tr in last 1 ch sp, 1 ch, 1 tr in top of turning ch, TURN.

Row 3: 3 ch, 2 tr in 1st 1 ch sp, * 1 ch, 3 tr in next 1 ch sp *; rep from * to * finishing with 3 tr in last sp, TURN.

Row 4: same as Row 2.

Lower Edge (shell edging)

Row 5: 1 sl st in 1st 1 ch sp, * 5 tr in 2nd tr of next 3 tr group, 1 sl st in next 1 ch sp *; rep from * to * finishing with 1 sl st in last sp.
Fasten off.

Upper Edge

With wrong side of towel facing you, use pencil and ruler to mark 32 dots equally spaced along upper edge of towel, starting and finishing 3 mm (⅛'') from each corner.

With right side of towel facing you, using 1.50 mm hook and 4 ply cotton, join yarn to upper edge of towel 3 mm (⅛'') from corner.

Row 1: 3 ch, 2 tr in same sp, * 1 ch, 3 tr in next dot (approximately 14 mm along edge) *; rep from * to * finishing with 3 tr in corner of towel, (32 groups of 3 tr) TURN.

Change to 2.00 mm hook.

Row 2: 4 ch, * miss 1 ch sp, (3 tr in next 1 ch sp, 1 ch) twice *; rep from * to * to last 1 ch sp, miss last 1 ch sp, 1 tr in top of turning ch, (20 groups of 3 tr). TURN.

Row 3: 3 ch, 2 tr in sp just formed, * miss 1 ch sp, (1 ch, 3 tr in next 1 ch sp) twice *; rep from * to * finishing with 3 tr in last sp, (14 groups of 3 tr). TURN.

Row 4: 4 ch, (miss 1 ch sp, 3 tr in next 1 ch sp, 1 ch) 6 times, miss 1 ch sp, 1 tr in top of turning ch, (6 groups of 3 tr). TURN.

Row 5: 3 ch, 2 tr in sp just formed, (miss 1 ch sp, 1 ch, 3 tr in next 1 ch sp) 3 times, (4 groups of 3 tr). TURN.

Row 6: (1 dc, 1 ch) in 1st tr, 1 tr in each of next 2 tr, (miss 1 ch sp, 1 tr in each of next 3 tr) 3 times, (12 tr). TURN.

Row 7: (1 dc, 1 ch) in 1st tr, 1 tr in each tr to end (12 tr). TURN.

Repeat Row 7 eleven times.

2nd last row: (1 dc, 1 ch) in 1st tr, 1 tr in each of next 3 tr, 4 ch, miss 4 tr, 1 tr in each of the rem 4 tr, (buttonhole formed), TURN.

Last row: (1 dc, 1 ch) in 1st tr, 1 tr in each of next 3 tr, 4 tr in 4 ch sp, 1 tr in each tr to end (12 tr).

Fasten off.

Upper Edge (shell edging)

With front of towel facing you, using 1.50 mm hook and 4 ply cotton, join yarn back into upper edge of towel in same sp as 1st 3 ch, 1 ch.

Change to 2.00 mm hook.

Along side edge of crochet, work 5 tr in centre of 1st 3 ch, 1 sl st in next sp, 5 tr in centre of next tr, 1 sl st in next sp, (5 tr in top of next tr, 1 sl st in top of next tr) 8 times, (YOU SHOULD BE AT THE CORNER) miss 1 tr, 7 tr in next tr, miss 2 tr, 1 sl st in each of next 2 tr, miss 2 tr, 7 tr in next tr, miss 1 tr, 1 sl st in corner tr; 5 tr in top of next tr, (1 sl st in top of next tr, 5 tr in top of next tr) 7 times, (1 sl st in next sp, 5 tr in centre of next tr) twice, change to 1.50 mm hook and work 1 sl st back into towel in last st.

Fasten off.

Button

Using 2.00 mm hook and 4 ply cotton make 4 ch, join with a sl st in 1st ch to form a ring; 1 ch, into centre ring work 7 dc, do not join with a sl st, (2 dc in next dc, 1 dc in each of next 2 dc) 6 times, 2 dc in next dc, 1 dc in each of next 14 dc (1 full round without shaping), (dec, 1 dc in next dc) 3 times, stuff firmly with cottonwool, (dec, 1 dc in next dc) 6 times, miss 1 dc, 1 sl st in next dc.

Fasten off by cutting cotton 30 cm (12") away from hook. Using the yarn attached to the button, sew button to front of upper edge (where the safety pin is).
Darn in all ends.

13 Lavender Bag

Materials
1.25 mm hook
No. 20 crochet cotton
lavender sachet
50 cm satin ribbon

Measurements: Lavender bag is heart-shaped, approximately 9 cm (3½'') long.

Instructions: Using No. 20 cotton and 1.25 mm hook work 15 ch, 1 sl st back into the 1st ch to form a ring.

Row 1: 4 ch, 39 dtr into ring, 1 sl st in top of 4th ch. ***

Row 2: 4 ch, 1 dtr into each of next 19 dtr. (20 dtr). TURN.

Row 3: 4 ch, into 1st dtr work (2 tr, 2 ch, 2 tr), 4 ch (for ribbon), * 1 dc into next dtr, 3 ch *; rep from * to * finishing with 1 dc in 2nd last dtr, 4 ch (for ribbon), into top of 4th ch work (2 tr, 2 ch, 2 tr). (seventeen 3 ch spaces). TURN.

> TIP: Shell over shell is when one shell is worked into the centre of the shell in the previous row.

Row 4: 4 ch, into next 2 ch sp work (2 tr, 2 ch, 2 tr)—this will now be called shell over shell, 4 ch, * 1 dc in next *3 ch sp*, 3 ch *; rep from * to * finishing with 1 dc in last 3 ch sp, 4 ch, shell over shell. (sixteen 3 ch spaces). TURN.

Row 5: 4 ch, shell over shell, 4 ch, * 1 dc in next *3 ch sp*, 3 ch *; rep from * to * finishing with 1 dc in last 3 ch sp, 4 ch, shell over shell. (fifteen 3 ch spaces). TURN.

Repeat Row 5 until you have only one 3 ch space left.

2nd last row: 4 ch, shell over shell, 4 ch, 1 dc in 3 ch sp, 4 ch, shell over shell. TURN.

Last row: 4 ch, 2 tr in centre of 1st shell, miss (4 ch, 1 dc, 4 ch), 2 tr in centre of 2nd shell, 4 ch, 1 sl st back in centre of 2nd shell. ***

Fasten off.

With front of 1st row facing you, using 1.25 mm hook and No. 20 cotton, join yarn to 1st dtr of remaining 20 dtr.

Repeat from *** to *** for other side.

Fasten off.
Darn in all loose ends.
Gently press on wrong side.

Using a piece of old stocking or fine fabric make a small sachet and fill with lavender. Slip sachet inside lavender bag and thread ribbon around. Fasten with a small bow at the top of the lavender bag.

GUIDE
With No. 20 cotton use 1.25 mm hook.
With No. 40 cotton use 1.00 mm hook.
With No. 60 cotton use 0.75 mm hook.

14 Handkerchief Edgings

I have chosen these designs because of their simplicity. Try working the edges in No. 40 cotton, as suggested, but as you become more confident progress to No. 60 cotton using .75 mm hook. No. 60 cotton, being finer, is mostly used for handkerchief edgings, although you will find it harder to see.

Lemon Edge

Materials
  1.00 mm hook
  No. 40 crochet cotton
  1 handkerchief with holes around edge

Preparation: with front of handkerchief facing you, using 1.00 mm hook and No. 40 cotton, join cotton to handkerchief in 2nd hole past corner, 1 ch.

Round 1: 1 dc in each hole around handkerchief working 3 dc in each corner hole, 1 sl st in 1st dc. ***

TIP: If you find the pattern does not quite work out at the end of the round, adjust the pattern around the corner so that it will work out. The reason we start just past the corner is to allow you to ease the pattern around the corner where it isn't as noticeable.

Round 2: 6 ch, 1 tr back into 1st dc, * miss 2 dc, (1 tr, 3 ch, 1 tr) in next dc *; rep from * to * around handkerchief working (1 tr, 3 ch, 1 tr, 3 ch, 1 tr) in each corner dc; 1 sl st in top of 3rd ch.

TIP: When you reach a corner stop and check your work. If correct continue on to next corner, but if incorrect, go back to your mistake and fix it up.

Round 3: 1 ch, * into next 3 ch loop work (3 dc, 3 ch, 3 dc) *; rep from * to * around handkerchief, finishing with 1 sl st in 1st dc.

Fasten off.
Darn in all loose ends, gently press on wrong side.

White Edge

Materials: same as for Lemon Edge.
Instructions: same as for Lemon Edge to end of Round 1. ***

Round 2: 1 ch, 1 dc back into 1st dc of Round 1, * 3 ch, miss 1 dc, 1 dc in next dc *; rep from * to * finishing with 1 sl st in 1st dc.

Round 3: 1 sl st in 1st 3 ch space, 3 ch, (2 tr, 3 ch, 3 tr) into same space, * miss next 3 ch sp, (3 tr, 3 ch, 3 tr) in next 3 ch sp *; rep from * to * finishing with 1 sl st in top of 3rd ch.
Fasten off.
Darn in all loose ends, gently press on wrong side.

Pink Edge

Materials: same as for Lemon Edge.
Instructions: same as for Lemon Edge to end of Round 1. ***

Round 2: 1 ch, 1 dc back into 1st dc of Round 1, 2 ch, 1 dc back into 1st dc of Round 1, * 5 ch, miss 2 dc, into next dc work (1 dc, 2 ch, 1 dc) *; rep from * to * finishing with 2 ch, 1 tr in 1st dc.

Round 3: 1 ch, (1 dc, 2 ch, 1 dc) in same loop, * 5 ch, (1 dc, 2 ch, 1 dc) in next loop *; rep from * to * finishing with 1 sl st in 1st dc.
Fasten off.
Darn in all loose ends, gently press on wrong side.

TIP: If possible, when working handkerchief edges, keep all corners similar.

These three diagrams show instructions for the same handkerchief edgings in graph form. Once you have mastered the written instructions, try working the same edge following the graph instead.

TIP: Always read graph work from right to left. ① indicates the begining of Round 1.

Lemon edge

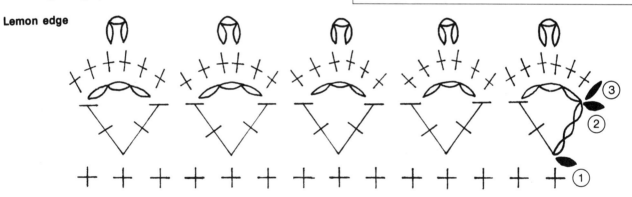

White edge

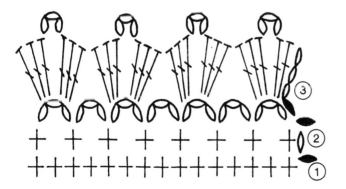

Pink edge

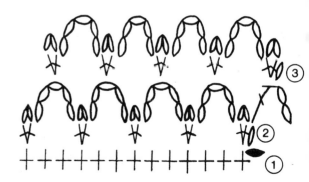

15 Handy Reference Guide

Abbreviation	Word	Symbol	Definition	Refer to
ch	chain	○	yarn over hook and draw through	Chapter 1 Chapter 2
sl st	slip stitch	●	hook into work, yarn over hook and draw through work and loop on hook (joining st)	Chapter 7
dc	double crochet	+	hook into work, yoh and draw through, yoh and draw through rem 2 loops on hook (*1 ch* for turning)	Chapter 3
htr	half treble	⊤	yoh, hook into work, yoh and draw through, yoh and draw through rem 3 loops on hook (*2 ch* for turning)	Chapter 7
tr	treble	⌐	yoh, hook into work, yoh and draw through, yoh and draw through 1st 2 loops on hook, yoh and draw through rem 2 loops on hook (*3 ch* or *1 dc, 1 ch* for turning)	Chapter 5
dtr	double treble	⌐	yoh twice, hook into work, yoh and draw through, (yoh and draw through next 2 loops on hook) twice, yoh and draw through rem 2 loops on hook (*4 ch* or *1 dc, 2 ch* for turning)	Chapter 7
tr tr	triple treble	⌐	yoh 3 times, hook into work, yoh and draw through, (yoh and draw through next 2 loops on hook) 3 times, yoh and draw through rem 2 loops on hook (*5 ch* or *1 dc, 3 ch* for turning)	Chapter 7
dec	decrease	✕✕ ⅄	to make 1 st only over 2 sts in work (hook into next st, yoh and draw through) twice, yoh and draw through rem 3 loops on hook (yoh, hook into next st, yoh and draw through, yoh and draw through 1st 2 loops on hook) twice, yoh and draw through rem 3 loops on hook	Chapter 8
inc	increase	✕✕ ⋎	to make 2 sts over only 1 st in work work 2 dc into the next st work 2 tr into the next st	Chapter 8

Abbreviation	Word	Definition
alt	alternate	every *alternate* row: every second row
approx	approximately	*approximately* 15 cm: near enough to 15 cm
beg	beginning	*beginning* of the row: start of the row
cont	continue	keep on going
foll	following	the *following* row: the next row
gp	group	a number of stitches all worked into the one place
lp	loop	rem 2 *loops* on hook: part of the stitch still on hook
		work into 5 ch *loop*: work into the space under the arch formed by the 5 chain
patt	pattern	follow the *pattern*: follow the written instructions
		repeat a *pattern*: a special instruction that may be repeated throughout, usually indicated by ***, or may be separately written at the start of the pattern
picot	picot	a number of ch joined at the base with either a sl st or a dc
rem	remaining	to *remaining* 3 sts: to the last 3 stitches left
rnd	round	to work in *rounds*: to work in a circle *Round 3:* an instruction worked in a circle
rep	repeat	work the same instruction over again
row	row	to work in a *row*: to work in a horizontal line
		Row 3: an instruction worked in a horizontal line
sp	space	miss 3 ch *space*: miss the arch formed by 3 chain
		work into next 4 ch *space*: work into the area under the 4 chain
st	stitch	the result after manoeuvring your hook: e.g. 1 dc, 1 tr, 1 dtr
tog	together	join *together*: join so as to unite
yoh	yarn over hook	the term used to describe wrapping the yarn around the hook